How do I use this scheme?

Key Words with Peter and Jane has three
parallel series, each containing twelve books. All three
series are written using the same carefully controlled
vocabulary. Readers will get the most out of **Key Words** with
Peter and Jane when they follow the books in the pattern
1a, 1b, 1c; 2a, 2b, 2c and so on.

• Series a
gradually introduces and repeats new words.

• Series b
provides further practice of these same words, but
in a different context and with different illustrations.

• Series c
uses familiar words to teach **phonics** in a methodical way,
enabling children to read increasingly difficult words.
It also provides a link to writing.

LADYBIRD BOOKS

UK | USA | Canada | Ireland | Australia
India | New Zealand | South Africa

Ladybird Books is part of the Penguin Random House group of companies
whose addresses can be found at global.penguinrandomhouse.com.

www.penguin.co.uk www.puffin.co.uk www.ladybird.co.uk

First published 1964
This edition 2009, 2014, 2016
Copyright © Ladybird Books Ltd, 1964
001

A CIP catalogue record for this book is
available from the British Library

ISBN: 978-1-409-30136-3

Printed in China

Key Words

with Peter and Jane

10c Learning is fun

written by W. Murray
illustrated by J.H. Wingfield

1 **sp**	2 **-y**	3 **-ed**
4 **tr**	5 **cr**	6 **-le**
7 **-mp**	8 **-oy**	9 **oi**
10 **-ir**	11 **-ur**	12 **-nk**
13 **br**	14 **-or**	

−ew

We know the words **new** and **few**.

Now we learn **yew, flew, stew, blew, chew** and **drew**.

1   Here is a yew tree. It is by a brick wall.

2   He opened the window, and the bee flew into the garden.

3   This is a mother in her kitchen. She is making a stew.

4   There are no leaves on this tree. The wind blew them down.

5   The boy is eating an apple. He likes something to chew.

6   The girl drew this picture. It is of her two brothers.

We know the words **black**, **blue** and **blow**.

Now we learn **blinks**, **blot**, **block**, **blank**, **blanket** and **blunt**.

1   The boy blinks in the sunlight.
    He has come out of a dark room.

2   As the girl writes with pen and ink,
    she makes a blot.

3   This man has a block of wood. He is
    going to make a small boat.

4   The paper is blank. The boy is
    thinking of something to write.

5   Mother brings another blanket as it is
    a cold night.

6   The saw is so blunt that it will not cut
    the wood.

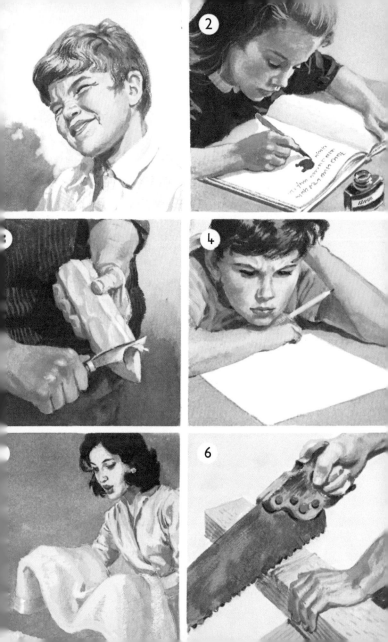

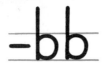

We know the words **rabbit** and **bubbles**.

Now we learn **nibbles, cabbage, scribbles, pebbles, rubber** and **ribbon**.

1   The rabbit nibbles. The boy gives it something to eat.

2   It nibbles some cabbage leaves from the garden. They are large leaves.

3   The baby boy scribbles. He does not know how to draw pictures.

4   The girl is by the sea. She throws pebbles into the water.

5   This is a ball. It is red and is made of rubber.

6   The girl has a coloured ribbon. She puts it in her hair.

ou

We know the words **out, outside, our, hour, round, found** and **about**.

Now we learn **sour, flour, shout, stout,** and **pound**.

1 The drink is sour. The boy does not like it.

2 The woman uses flour. She is making a cake.

3 The man shouts to the boys. They hear his shout.

4 The man is stout. He is not very tall but he is heavy.

5 The old man owns a boat. He is about to paint it.

6 The girl buys a pound of apples. She likes to shop for her mother.

1

2

3

4

5

6

-ew bl -bb ou

Choose the correct words from the
right-hand list to complete each numbered
sentence. The pictures will help you.

1 There are three | a cabbage leaf.

2 The boy chews | in her hair.

3 He blinks | to make a cake.

4 She brings a blanket | an apple.

5 A rabbit nibbles | yew trees.

6 She has a ribbon | as it is cold.

7 The man is about | in the sunlight.

8 She uses flour | to paint a boat.

The answers are on Page 48.

-SS

We know the words **dress**, **dressed**, **dressing**, **grass**, **cross**, **across** and **message**.

Now we learn **class**, **glass**, **kiss**, **chess**, **moss**, and **missed**.

1   The girl is at school. She sits with her class.

2   A boy broke this glass with a ball. The man will mend it.

3   The mother loves her baby. She gives him a kiss.

4   The boys can play chess. They learn it at school.

5   There is moss on the wall. It is an old wall.

6   The girl tried to catch the ball but she missed it.

gr

We know the words **green, grass, grandmother** and **grandfather**.

Now we learn **grows, grain, grapes, grunt, grate** and **ground**.

1 The girl grows flowers. She picks some of them.

2 The farmer has a large sack. There is grain in it.

3 This man grows grapes in his garden. They are green.

4 The pigs grunt as they eat their food. They are large and black.

5 There is a fire in the grate. A cat sits by the fire.

6 Here is an apple tree. There are apples under it, on the ground.

-igh

We know the words **right**, **night**, **fight**, and **light**.

Now we learn **flight**, **bright**, **high**, **lightning**, **sight** and **tight**.

1 The children have a flight in an aeroplane. They like to fly.

2 The sun is bright and hot. It is a summer day.

3 There is a bird high in a tree. It is a large bird.

4 There is a storm. Lightning is flashing in the sky.

5 This man's sight is not good. He has a white stick.

6 He says that the coat is tight. It is too small for him.

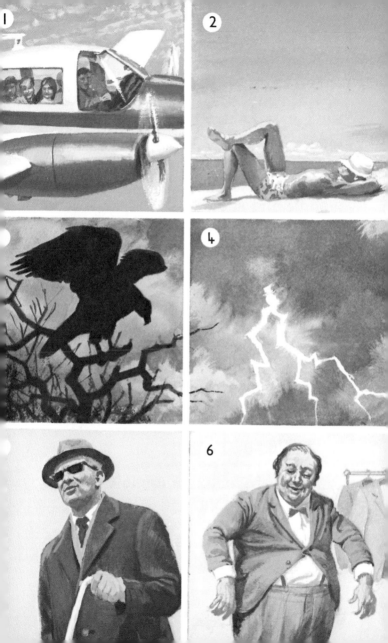

We know the words **daddy**, **paddles**, **saddle** and **puddle**.

Now we learn **add**, **odd**, **ladder**, **muddy**, **muddle** and **cuddle**.

1   The boys add up the numbers.
    Their answers are right.

2   The girl writes down odd numbers.
    She writes one, three and five.

3   The man climbs up to the window
    with a long ladder.

4   The boy is muddy. He has been
    playing in the rain.

5   The baby makes a muddle in his
    mother's room.

6   The mother holds her baby. She
    gives him a cuddle.

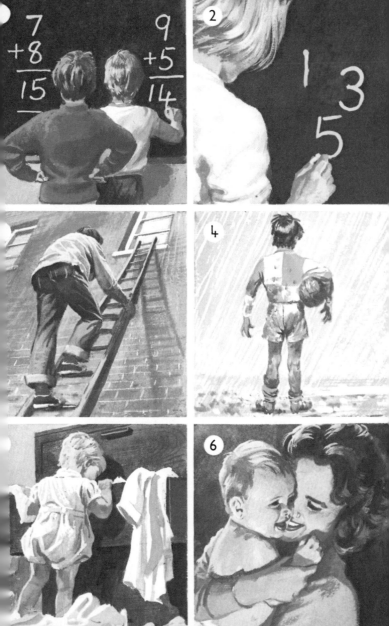

gr –igh –dd –ss

Complete the sentences as you write them in your exercise book. The pictures will help you.

1 The boy likes to help his --andfather.
He has cut the --ass for him.
His --andfather gives him some
--apes.

2 Her mother gives the girl a ribbon.
It is br---t red.
She ties the ribbon t---tly.

3 The boy is very young. He pa--les
in a pu--le and gets mu--y.

4 He tried to catch the kite with his
hand but he mi--ed it.

The answers are on Page 48.

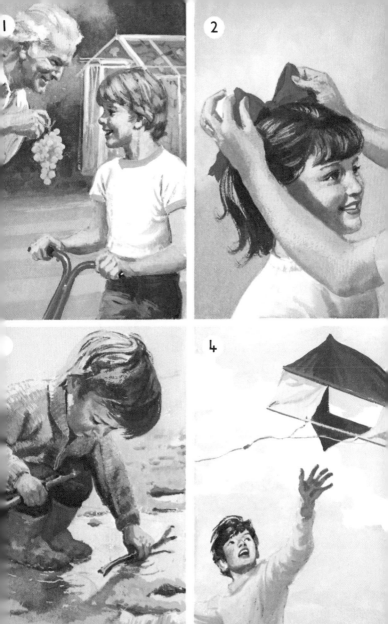

-rr

We know the words **arrange**, **mirror**, **lorry** and **worry**.

Now we learn **purrs**, **berries**, **merry**, **carries**, **married** and **sorry**.

1   The cat likes the girl. It sits and purrs.

2   She has leaves and berries to put in the vase.

3   The man likes to laugh a lot. He is a merry man.

4   The boy helps the old lady. He carries her bag.

5   The man and woman are being married in the church.

6   The dog has hurt its paw. The boy is sorry for it.

1

2

4

6

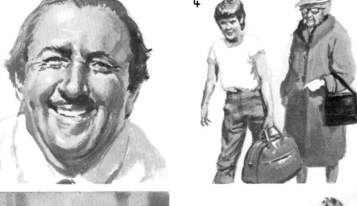

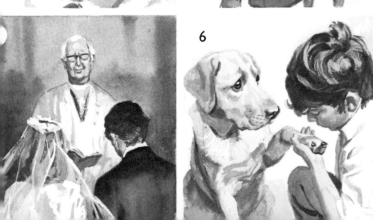

#

We know the words **pier** and **piece**.

Now we learn **fierce, shrieks, chief, handkerchief, niece** and **field**.

1 The man has a dog. It looks fierce and wants to fight the cat.

2 When this girl sees the mice she shrieks and jumps on the chair.

3 This is an Indian chief. He rides without a saddle.

4 The boy has a cold in the head and uses a large handkerchief.

5 The woman is the aunt of the girl. The girl is her niece.

6 This man puts his horse in the field and shuts the gate.

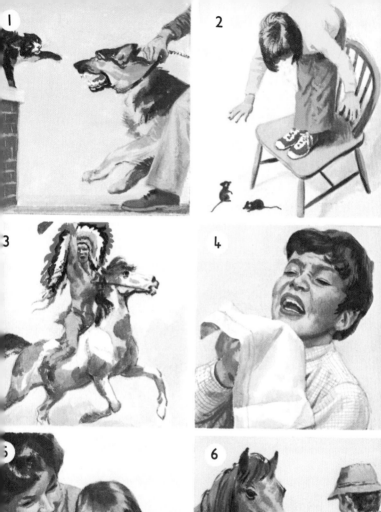

-nn

We know the words **dinner**, **funny** and **sunny**.

Now we learn **inn**, **penny**, **running**, **winning**, **tennis** and **sunning**.

1   Here is an inn. You can stop here for food and drink.

2   The boy has a coin. It is a ten penny piece. It will buy a few sweets.

3   This boy is running. He is in a race with some other boys.

4   He is winning the race. He comes in before any of the others.

5   This girl plays tennis. She is by the net as she hits the ball.

6   It is a sunny summer day. She is sunning herself.

The silent k

The letter k is silent in these words—
**knows, knit, knee, knob, knocks, kneels,
knife.**

1   The girl knows how to knit. She is
    knitting a sock.

2   The boy hurt his knee at games. The
    nurse is looking at it.

3   His hand is on the door. He holds the
    door knob.

4   The postman knocks at the door.
    He brings some birthday presents.

5   The man kneels to work on his car.
    There is something wrong with it.

6   The boy has a knife. He uses it to cut a
    stick.

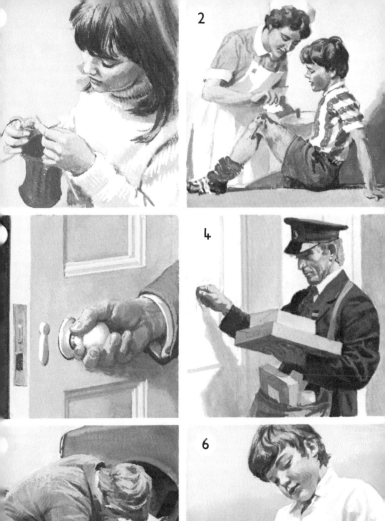

-rr silent k -ie -nn

Choose the correct words from the
right-hand list to complete each numbered
sentence. The pictures will help you.

1	The man and woman	a sock.
2	The girl picks	with a knife.
3	She is knitting	wants to fight.
4	He cuts a stick	a race.
5	The horse in the field	at the inn.
6	The fierce dog	have been married.
7	The men have a drink	some berries.
8	The boy is running	looks over the gate.

The answers are on Page 49.

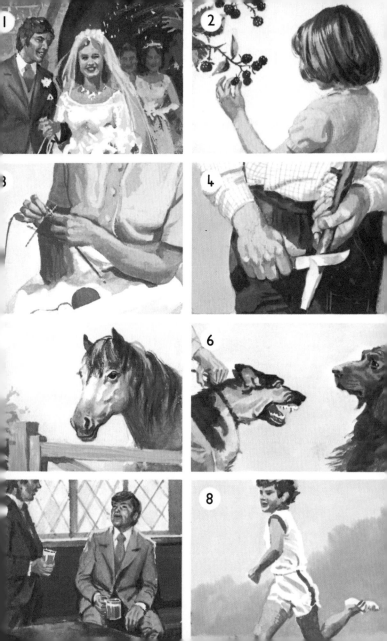

An accident

The man was on the high wire at the circus. Peter and Jane were in the great crowd which had come to watch. "It gives me a funny feeling to see a man so far up," said Jane to her brother.

"Yes," answered Peter, "the wire is so thin. He could easily fall." Just then the man slipped off the wire. A few people shrieked as he fell downwards. He fell into the net below and bounced up and down. "He's bouncing like a rubber ball," said Peter. "I'm so glad he's safe."

Copy out and complete —

1 Peter and Jane were in the - - eat crowd.
2 Jane said she had a fu - - y feeling.
3 The man fell from the h - - - wire.
4 A f - - people shr - - ked as he fell.
5 The man fell into the n - t.
6 He bounced like a ru - - er ball.

The answers are on Page 49.

A fire

The large house was on fire and some people were trapped inside. Smoke and fire were coming out of the windows. A fire engine soon arrived and a fireman put a ladder up to a window where a girl in a blue dress could be seen. He knew just what to do. He climbed the ladder and pulled the girl out of the building. Then he carried her down to the ground.

The firemen saved all the other people who were trapped in the house. They put out the fire with water. They worked quickly and were very brave.

Copy out and complete —

1 A fire engine soon a--ived at the fire.
2 A fireman put a la--er up to a window.
3 The girl was in a --ue dre--.
4 The fireman -new what to do.
5 He pulled the girl --t of the building.
6 He ca--ied her down to the --ound.

The answers are on Page 50.

Rescue at sea

A man was at sea in a boat in a great storm. The wind blew very hard and the waves were high. The boat was tossed about. Then it filled with water, turned over and floated upside down. The man fell into the water but he climbed onto the bottom of the boat.

Two men in a helicopter saw him. They flew low over the boat and let down a rope for him to hold. Then they pulled him up into the helicopter. He was wet but safe. He thanked the two men very much.

Copy out and complete —

1 It was a --eat storm.
2 The wind --ew very hard.
3 The waves were h---.
4 The boat was to--ed ab--t.
5 The helicopter fl-- low.
6 The man from the b--t was saved.

The answers are on Page 50.

A flood

There was very heavy rain for a long time. The river overflowed its banks and water covered the fields by the inn. It rose higher and higher until the ground floor rooms of the inn were under water. All the people in the inn went to one of the bedrooms.

Then some men in a rubber raft came to the rescue. They knelt in the raft and paddled it close to the window. The people climbed into the raft and were saved. A kennel floated by with a dog on it. A man in the rubber raft lifted the dog into the raft.

Copy out and complete —

1 Flood water covered the f - - lds.
2 The water rose h - - - er and h - - - er.
3 Water came into the i - -.
4 The - - ound floor rooms were under water.
5 Men came in a ru - - er raft.
6 They - nelt in the raft to pa - - le.

The answers are on Page 50.

Buying a puppy

The farmer had a few puppies to sell and he showed them to a man he knew. This man wanted one for his little girl.

The puppies were asleep on a blanket and some straw in a corner of a barn. One woke up and tried to nibble a biscuit. Then the others woke up and the farmer carried them out to a field where they could run about. The girl and her father watched the puppies running across the grass and playing together.

It was not long before the little girl was on her way home with her new puppy.

Copy out and complete —

1 The farmer had a f - - puppies.
2 He showed them to a man he - new.
3 The puppies were asleep on a - - anket.
4 One puppy tried to ni - - le a biscuit.
5 He ca - - ied them - - t to a f - - ld.
6 They were ru - - ing acro - - the gra - -.

The answers are on Page 51.

The clowns

Peter and Jane went to the circus with their grandfather. They saw men on the high trapeze fly through the air, and daring riders stand on the saddles of galloping horses. They saw elephants and sea lions and a dancing bear.

Then the clowns came in. They knew just how to make children laugh. The boys and girls shrieked with laughter as the two funny men ran about the ring and did their tricks.

The children laughed most of all as one clown blew bubbles and the other poured water into his baggy trousers.

Copy out and complete —

1 --andfather took the children to the circus.
2 They saw men on the h--- trapeze.
3 There were horse riders who stood on sa--les.
4 The clowns -new how to make children laugh.
5 The clowns did fu--y tricks.
6 One clown --ew bu--les.

The answers are on Page 51.

Pages 48 to 51 give the answers to the written exercises in this book.

Page 14

1 There are three yew trees.

2 The boy chews an apple.

3 He blinks in the sunlight.

4 She brings a blanket as it is cold.

5 A rabbit nibbles a cabbage leaf.

6 She has a ribbon in her hair.

7 The man is about to paint a boat.

8 She uses flour to make a cake.

Page 24

1 The boy likes to help his grandfather.
He has cut the grass for him.
His grandfather gives him some grapes.

2 Her mother gives the girl a ribbon.
It is bright red.
She ties the ribbon tightly.

3 The boy is very young.
He paddles in a puddle and gets muddy.

4 He tried to catch the kite with his hand but he missed it.

Page 34

1 The man and woman have been married.

2 The girl picks some berries.

3 She is knitting a sock.

4 He cuts a stick with a knife.

5 The horse in the field looks over the gate.

6 The fierce dog wants to fight.

7 The men have a drink at the inn.

8 The boy is running a race.

Page 36

1 Peter and Jane were in the great crowd.

2 Jane said she had a funny feeling.

3 The man fell from the high wire.

4 A few people shrieked as he fell.

5 The man fell into the net.

6 He bounced like a rubber ball.

Page 38

1   A fire engine soon arrived at the fire.

2   A fireman put a ladder up to a window.

3   The girl was in a blue dress.

4   The fireman knew what to do.

5   He pulled the girl out of the building.

6   He carried her down to the ground.

Page 40

1   It was a great storm.

2   The wind blew very hard.

3   The waves were high.

4   The boat was tossed about.

5   The helicopter flew low.

6   The man from the boat was saved.

Page 42

1   Flood water covered the fields.

2   The water rose higher and higher.

3   Water came into the inn.

4   The ground floor rooms were under water.

5   Men came in a rubber raft.

6   They knelt in the raft to paddle.

Page 44

1   The farmer had a few puppies.

2   He showed them to a man he knew.

3   The puppies were asleep on a blanket.

4   One puppy tried to nibble a biscuit.

5   He carried them out to a field.

6   They were running across the grass.

Page 46

1   Grandfather took the children to the circus.

2   They saw men on the high trapeze.

3   There were horse riders who stood on their saddles.

4   The clowns knew how to make children laugh.

5   The clowns did funny tricks.

6   One clown blew bubbles.

Revision of sounds
learned in this book

-ew bl -bb ou -ss
gr -igh -dd -rr
-ie -nn k(silent)

Learning by sounds

If children learn the sounds of letters and how to blend them with the other letter sounds (eg. c-a-t) they can tackle new words independently (eg. P-a-t).

In the initial stages it is best if these phonic words are already known to the learner.

However, not all English words can be learned in this way as the English language is not purely phonetic (eg. t-h-e).

In general a 'mixed' approach to reading is recommended. Some words are learned by blending the sounds of their letters and others by look-and-say, whole word or sentence methods.

This book provides the link with writing for the words in Readers 10a and 10b.